This is the story of Penguiy. I hope you enjoy this fun coloring book.

As you follow him along on his adventures and learn about his life, do not forget to take

out your
crayons,
markers, or
color pencils
and have fun!

Thank you so much and as Penguiy always says, eat a healthy meal and have

plenty of hugs
and snugs!

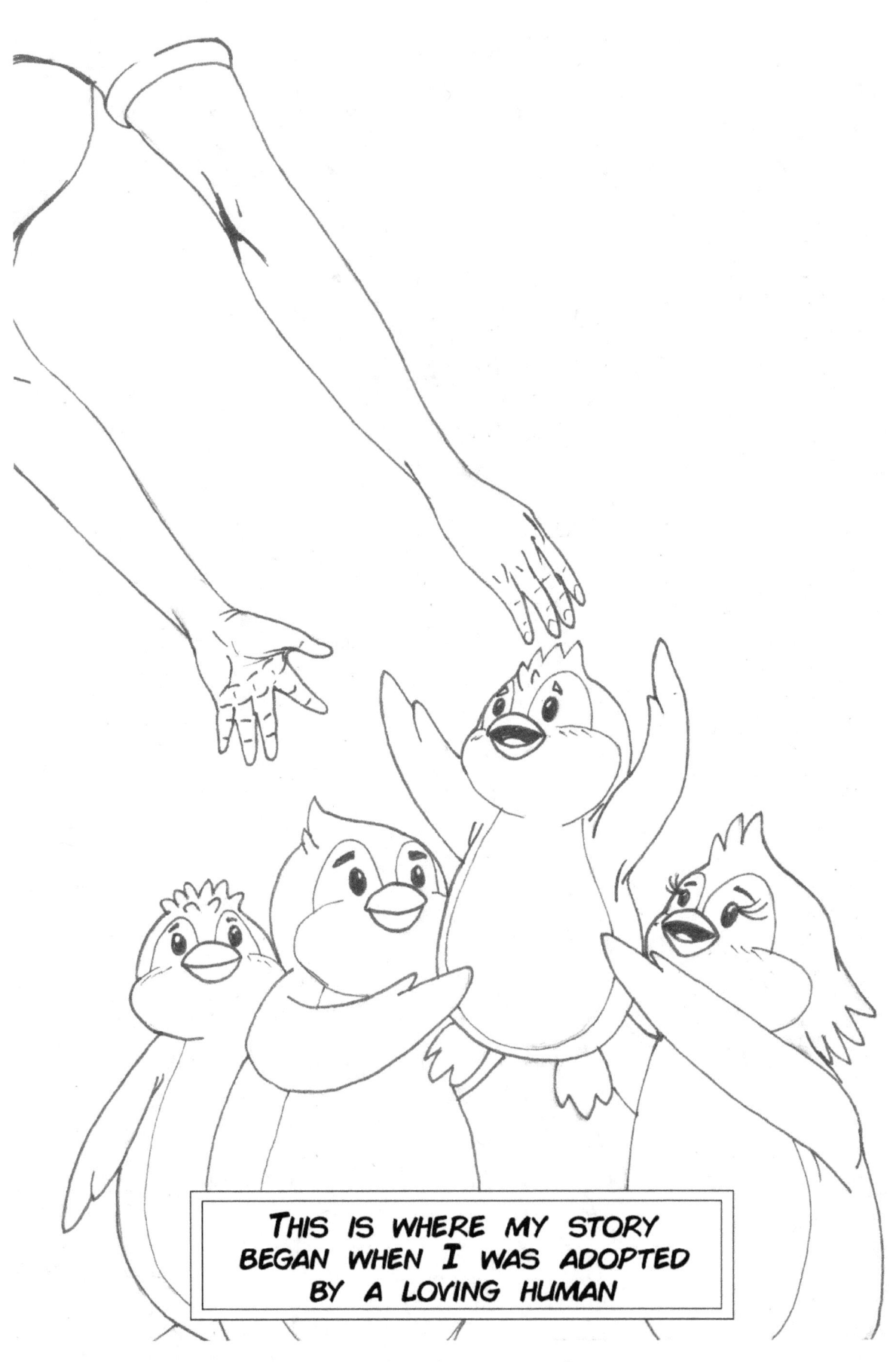

THIS IS WHERE MY STORY BEGAN WHEN I WAS ADOPTED BY A LOVING HUMAN

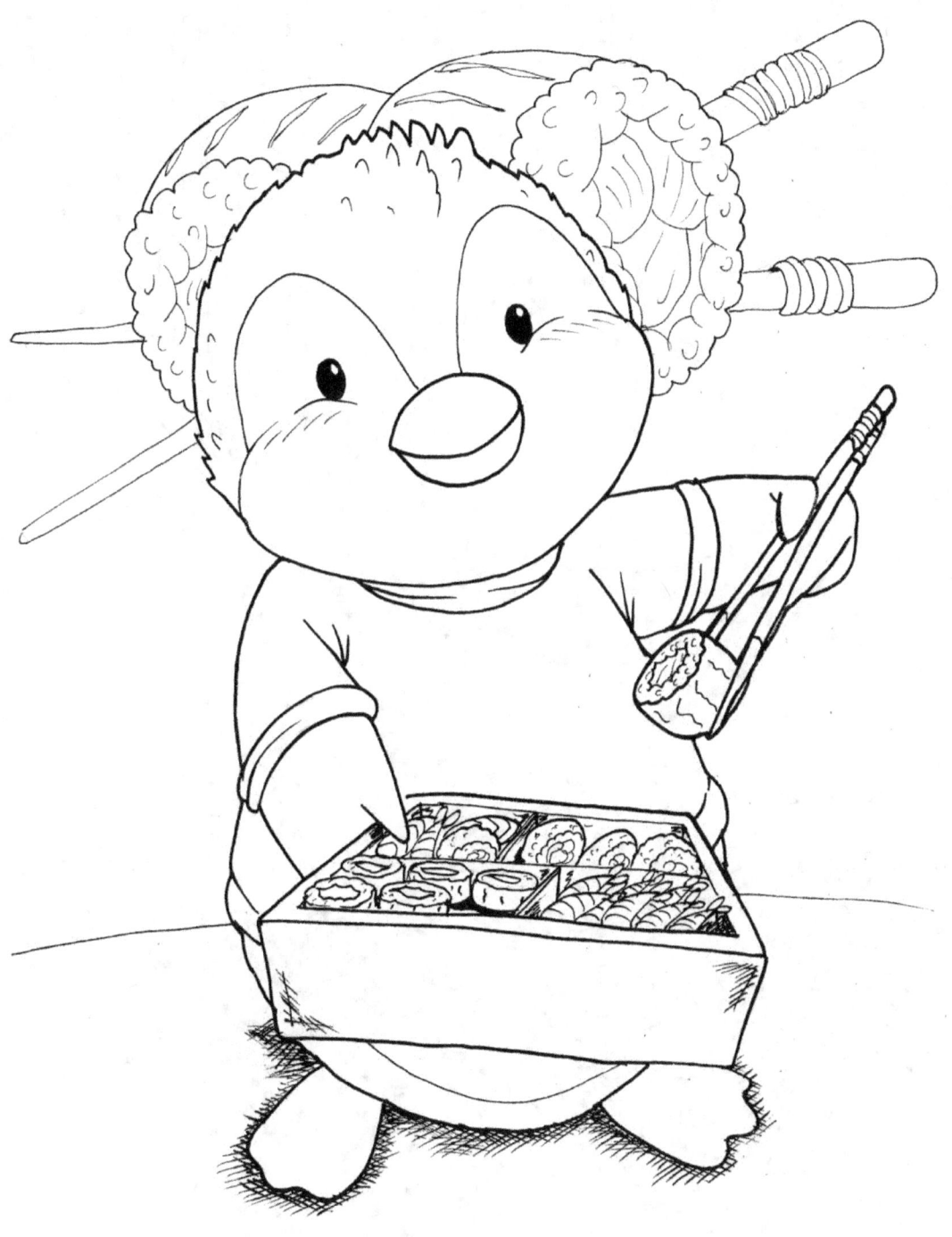

I LOVE TO EAT A
NICE SUSHI TREAT

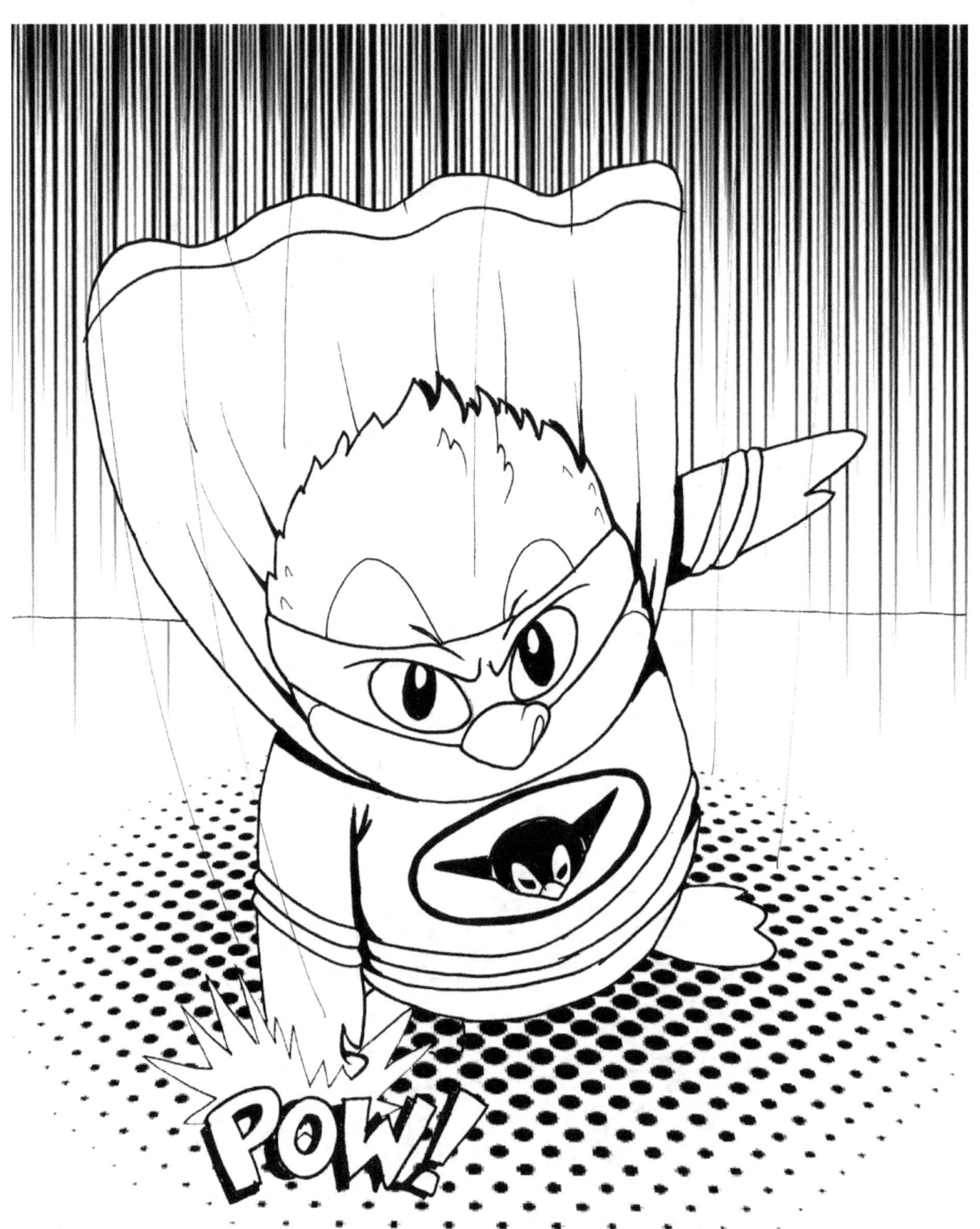

MY SECRET SUPERHERO IDENTITY
IS BatPenguiy

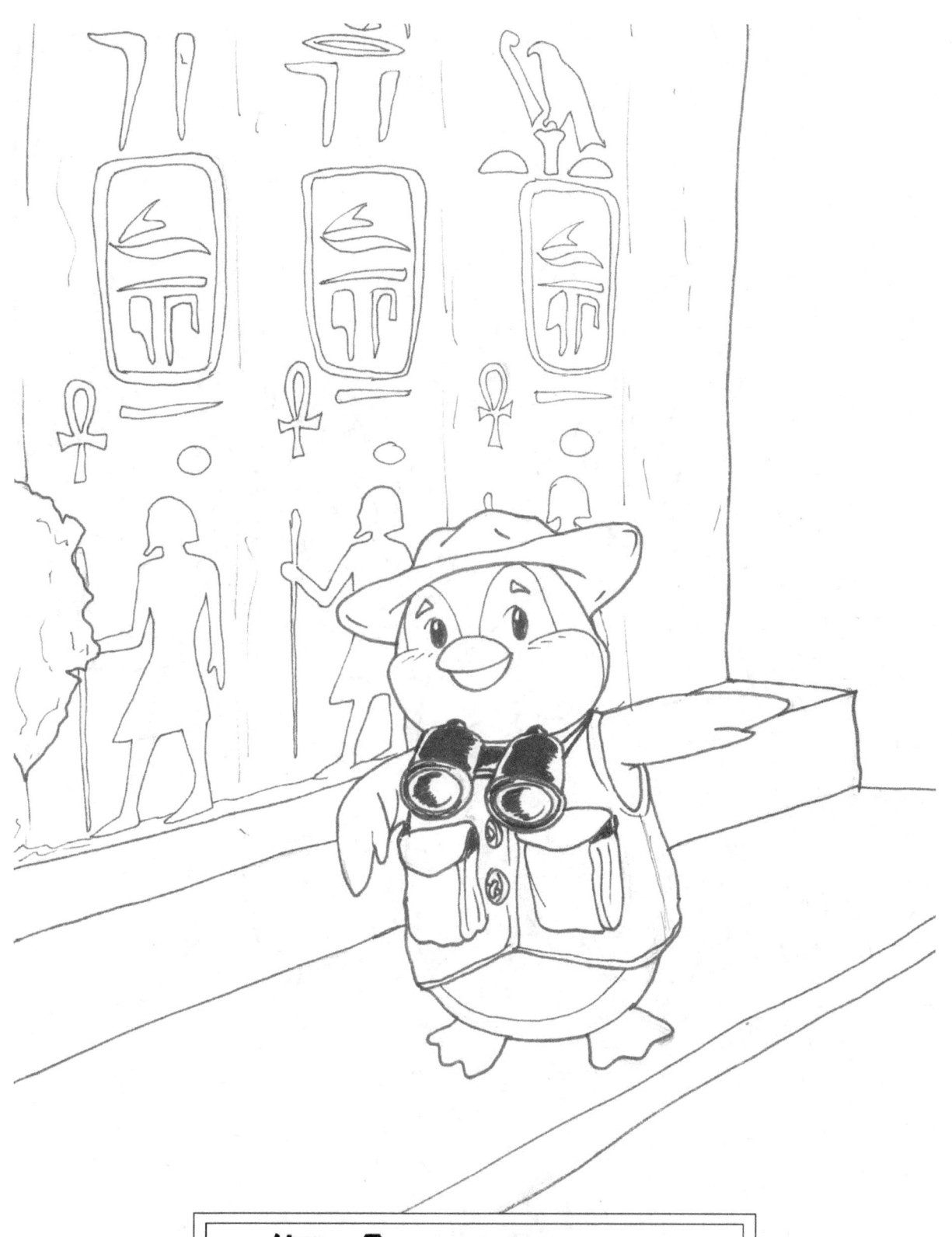

HERE I AM CHECKING OUT
HISTORY AND TRYING TO
SOLVE A MYSTERY

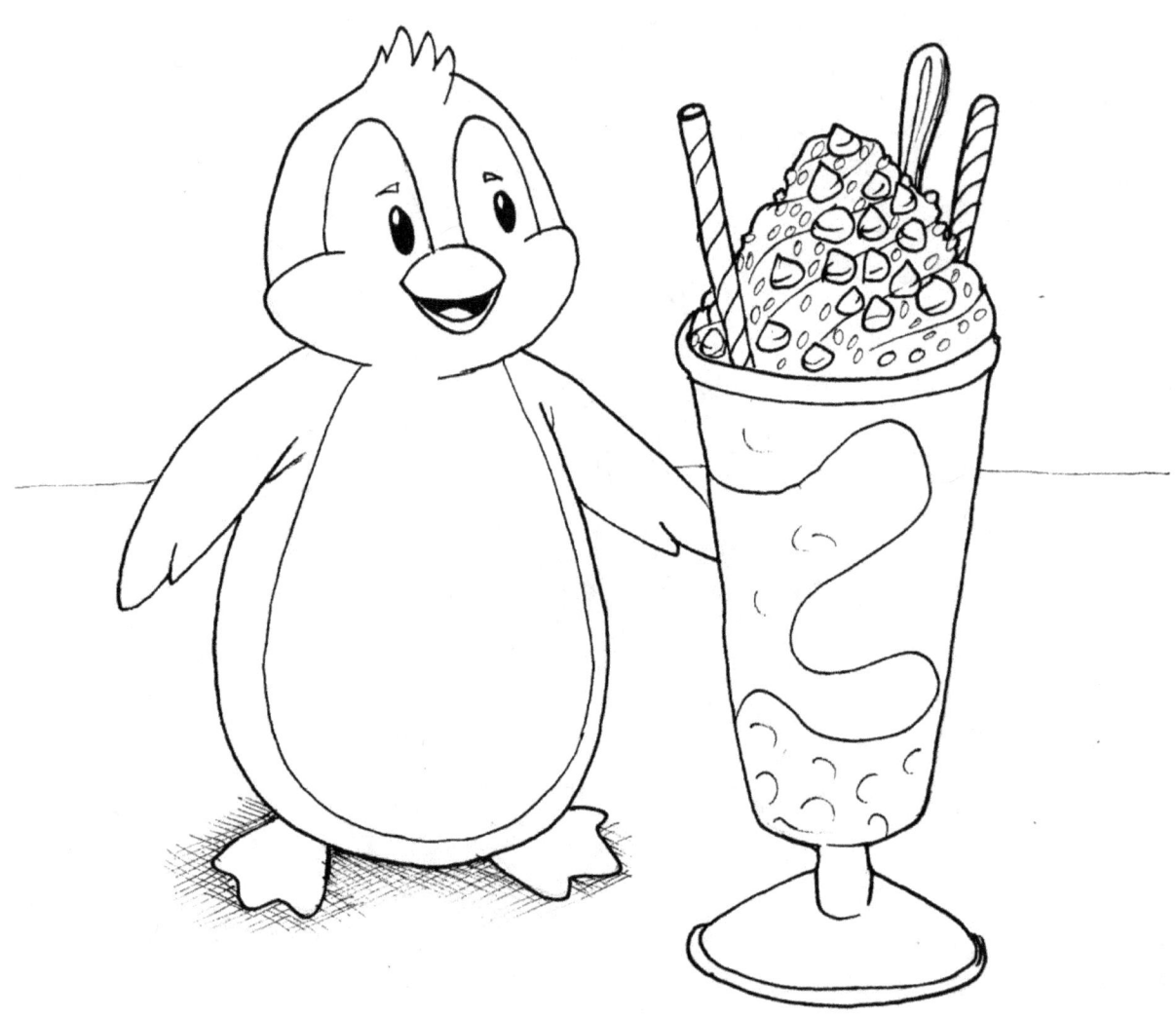

I LIKE TO EAT VEGAN ICE CREAM
HAVING IT IS LIKE A DREAM

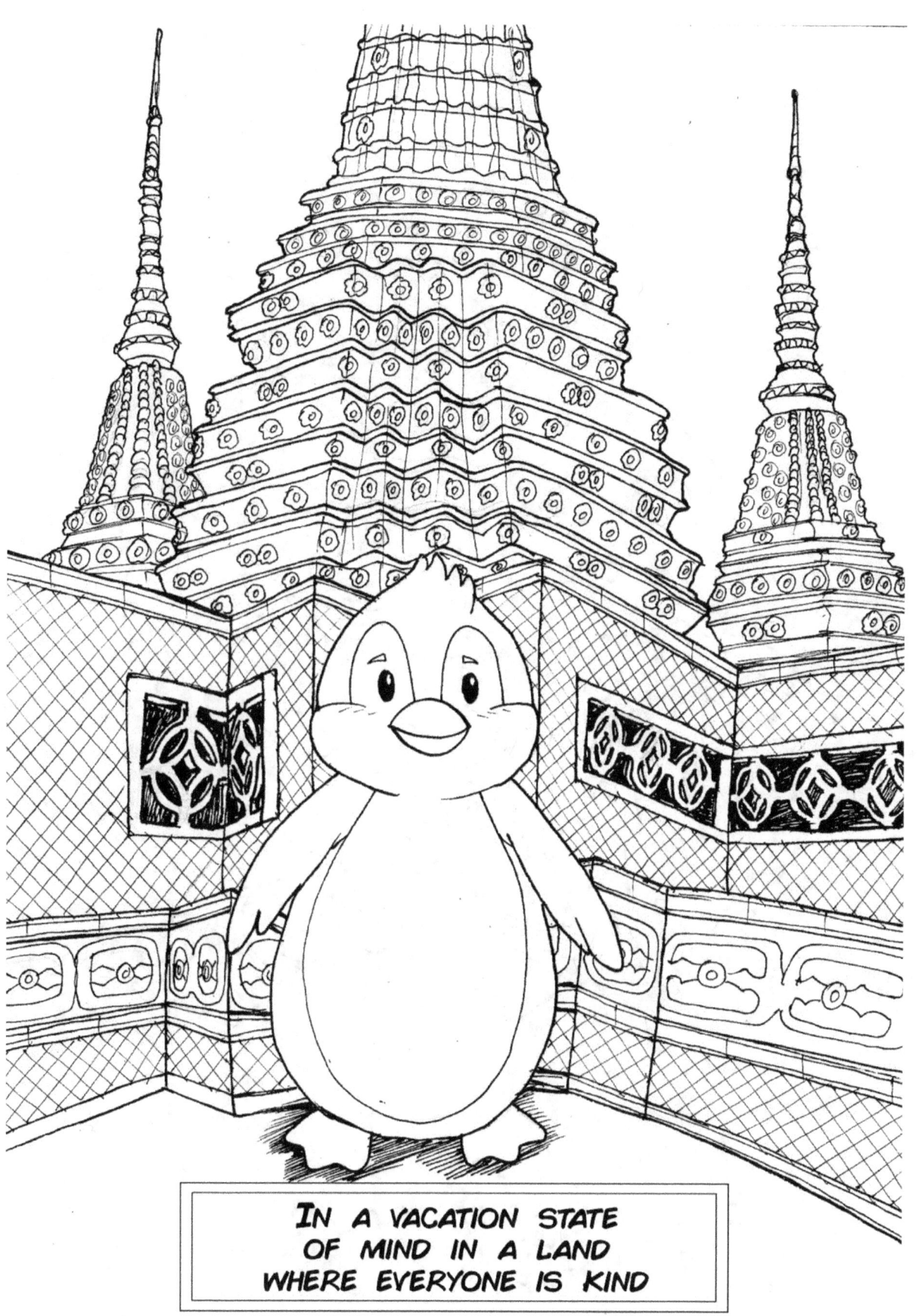

IN A VACATION STATE
OF MIND IN A LAND
WHERE EVERYONE IS KIND

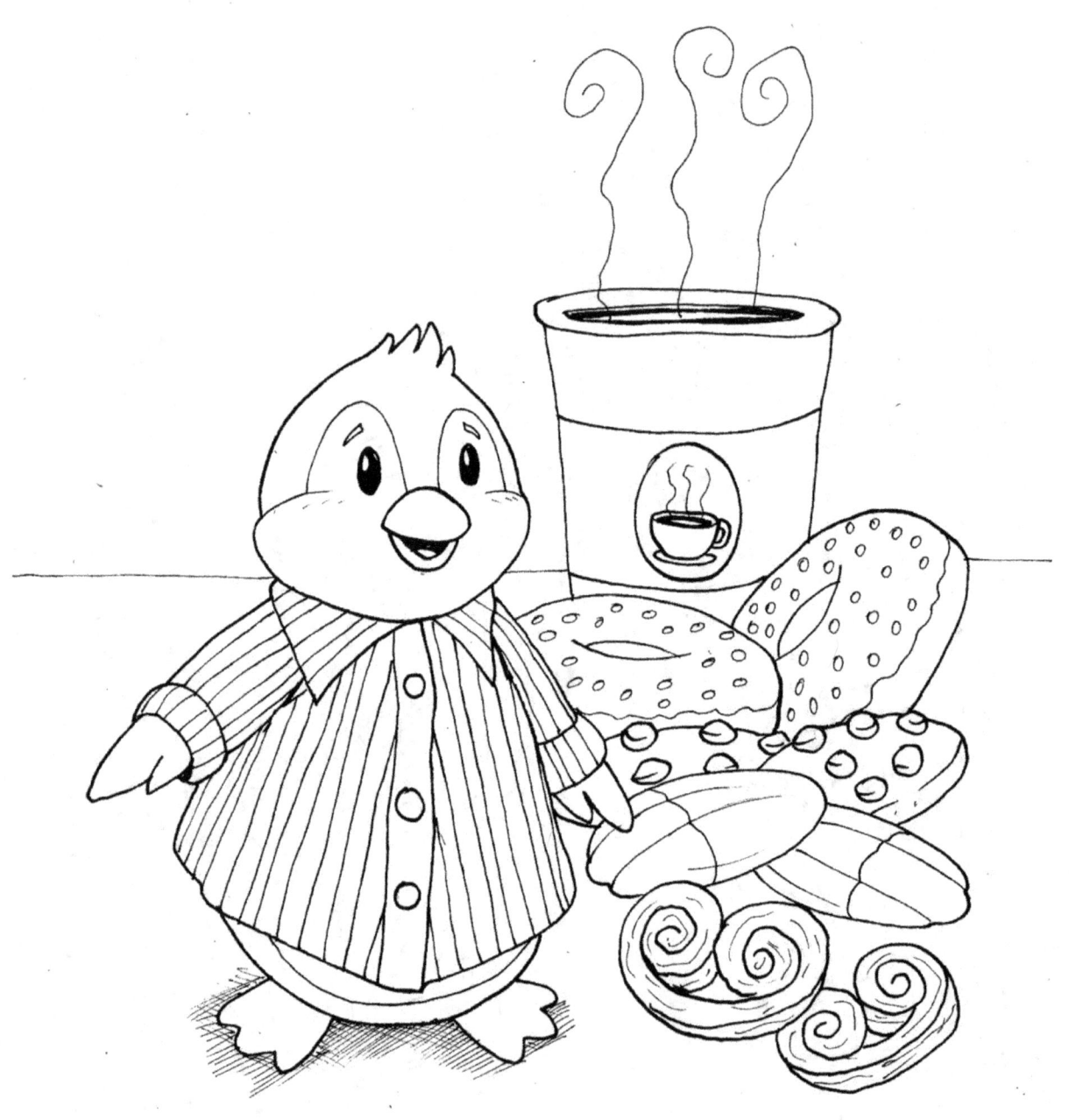

I LIKE MY BREAKFAST A LITTLE
SWEET MAKES ME FEEL LIKE
HAPPY FEET

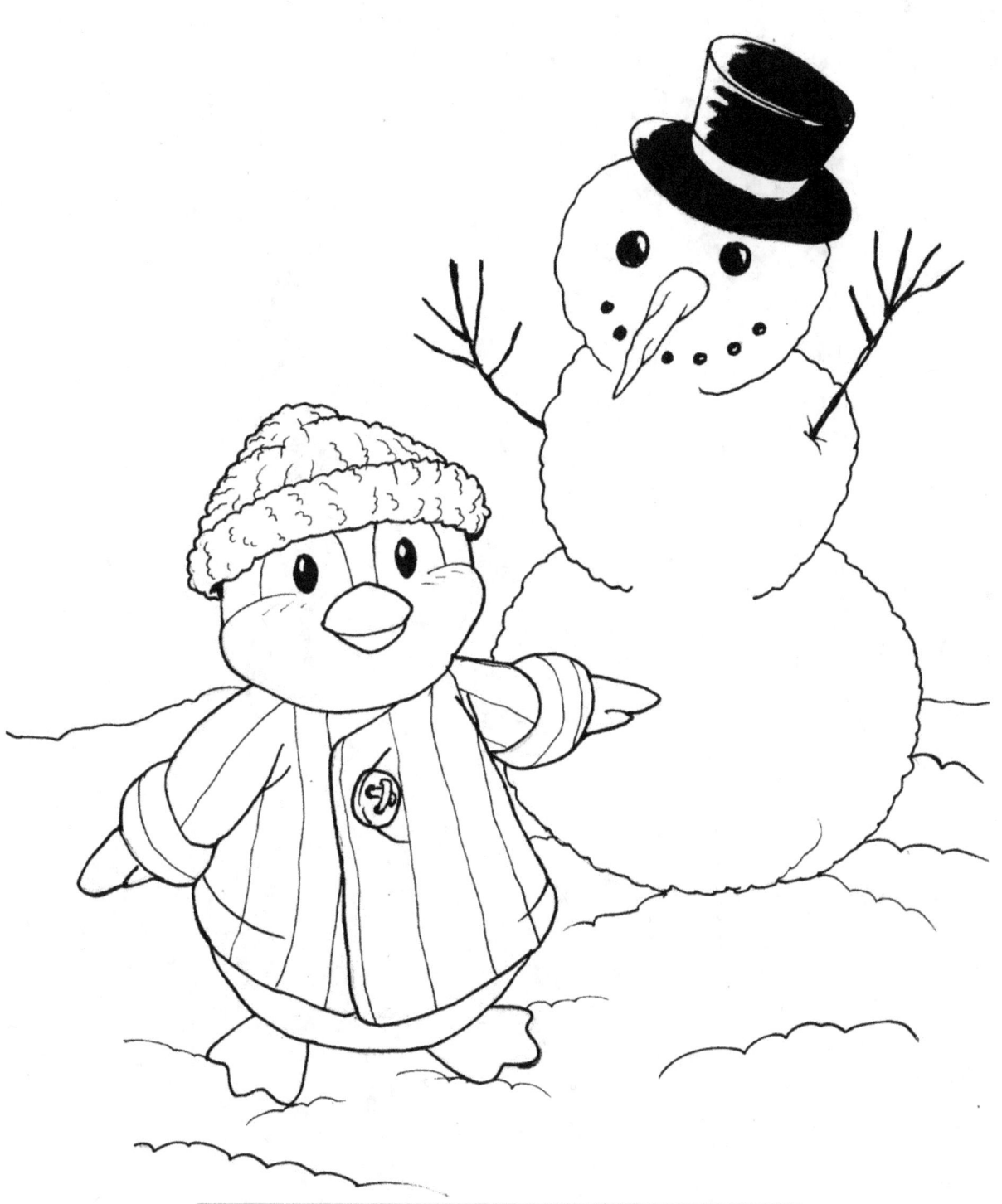

I LIKE TO PLAY IN THE SNOW,
IT GIVES ME A LITTLE GLOW

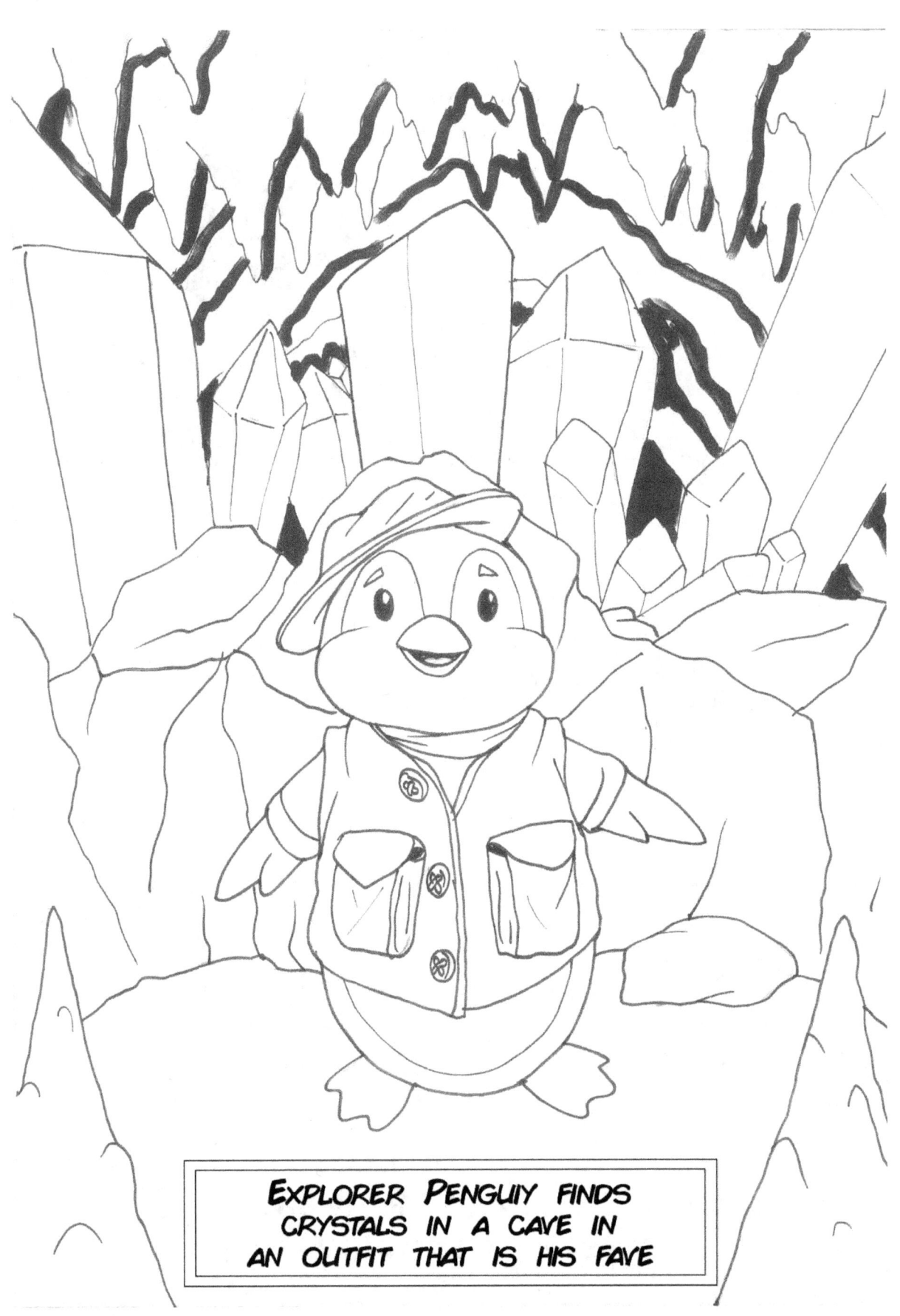

EXPLORER PENGUIY FINDS
CRYSTALS IN A CAVE IN
AN OUTFIT THAT IS HIS FAVE

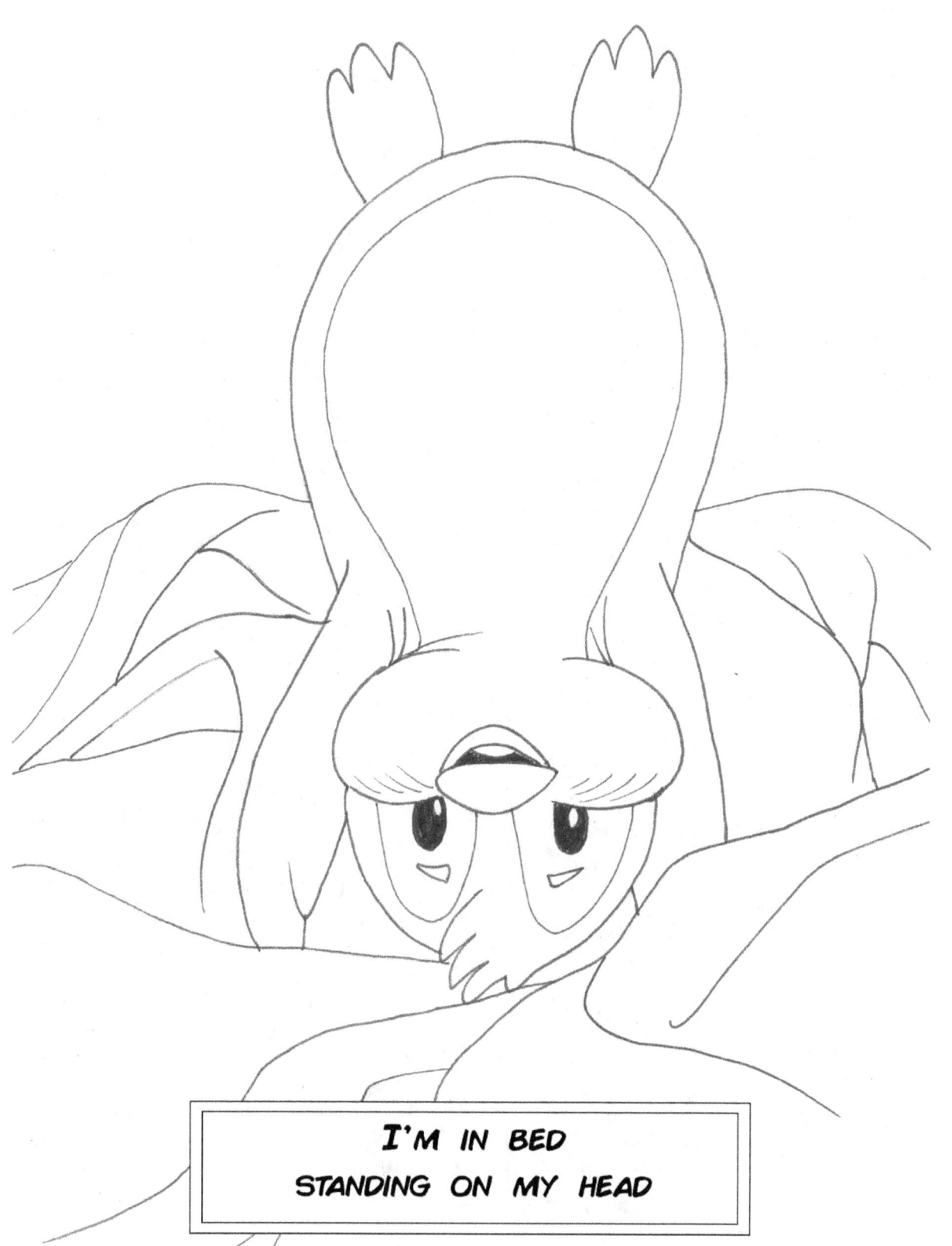

I'M IN BED
STANDING ON MY HEAD

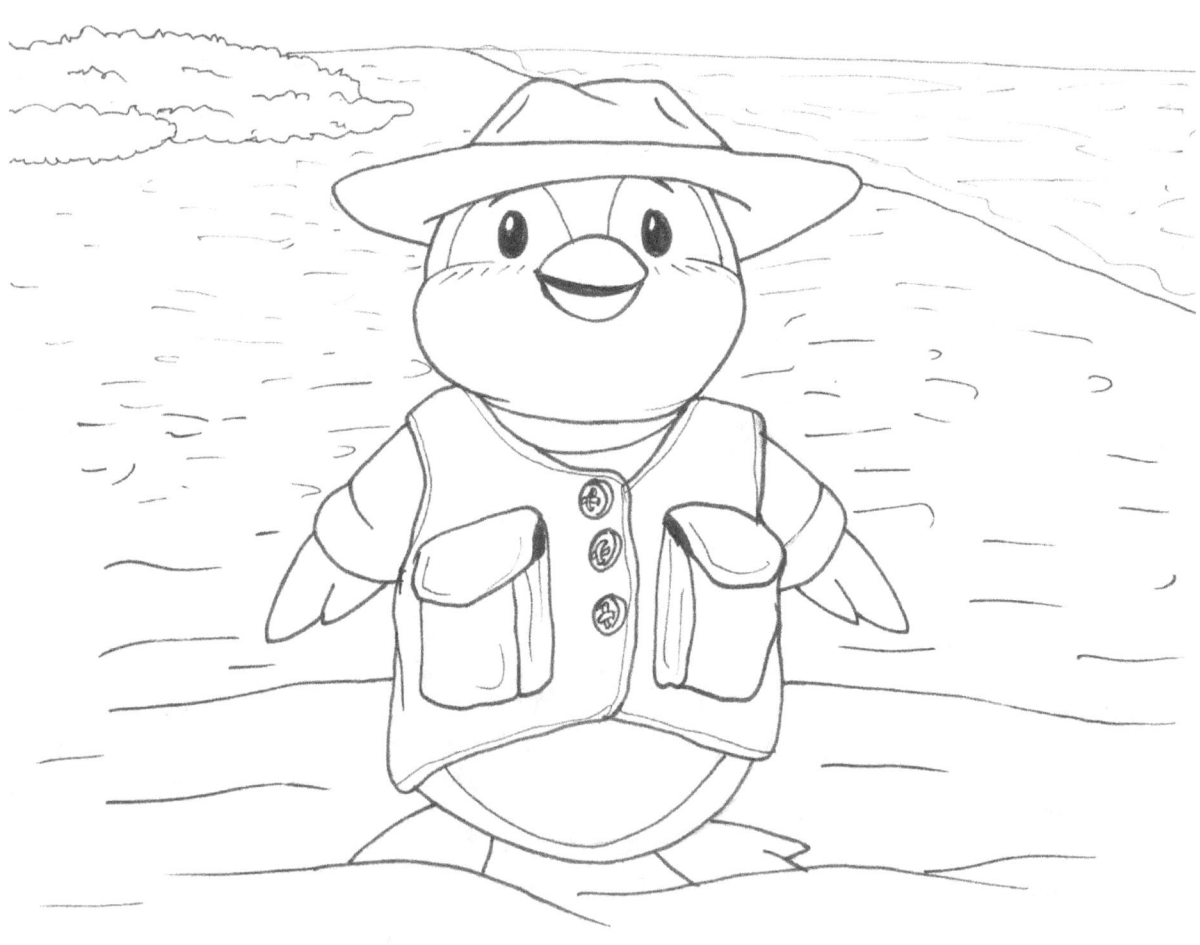

HERE I AM LOOKING FOR
TREASURE IN THE SAND
WHILE BENEATH A SUNSET
EVER SO GRAND

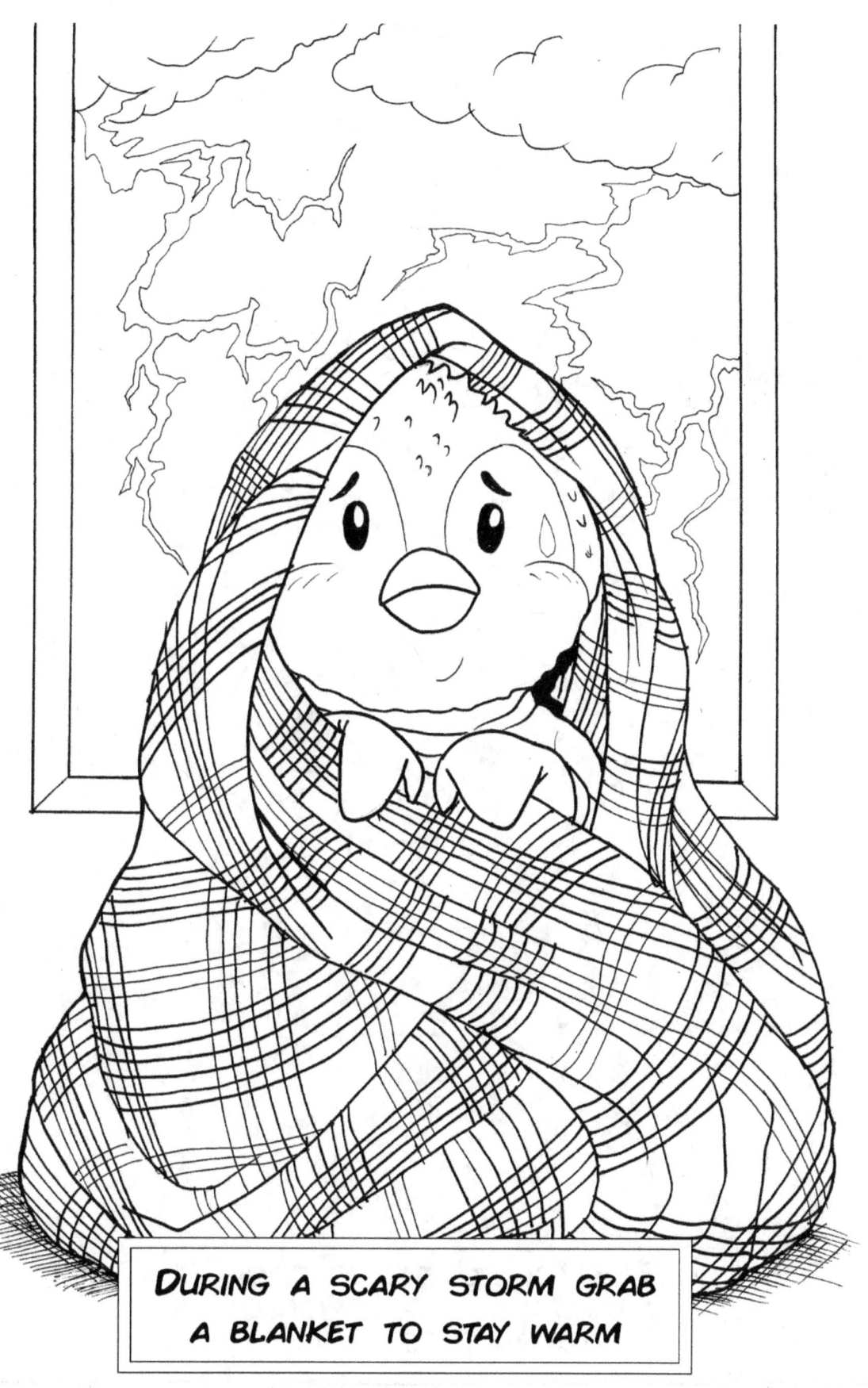

DURING A SCARY STORM GRAB
A BLANKET TO STAY WARM

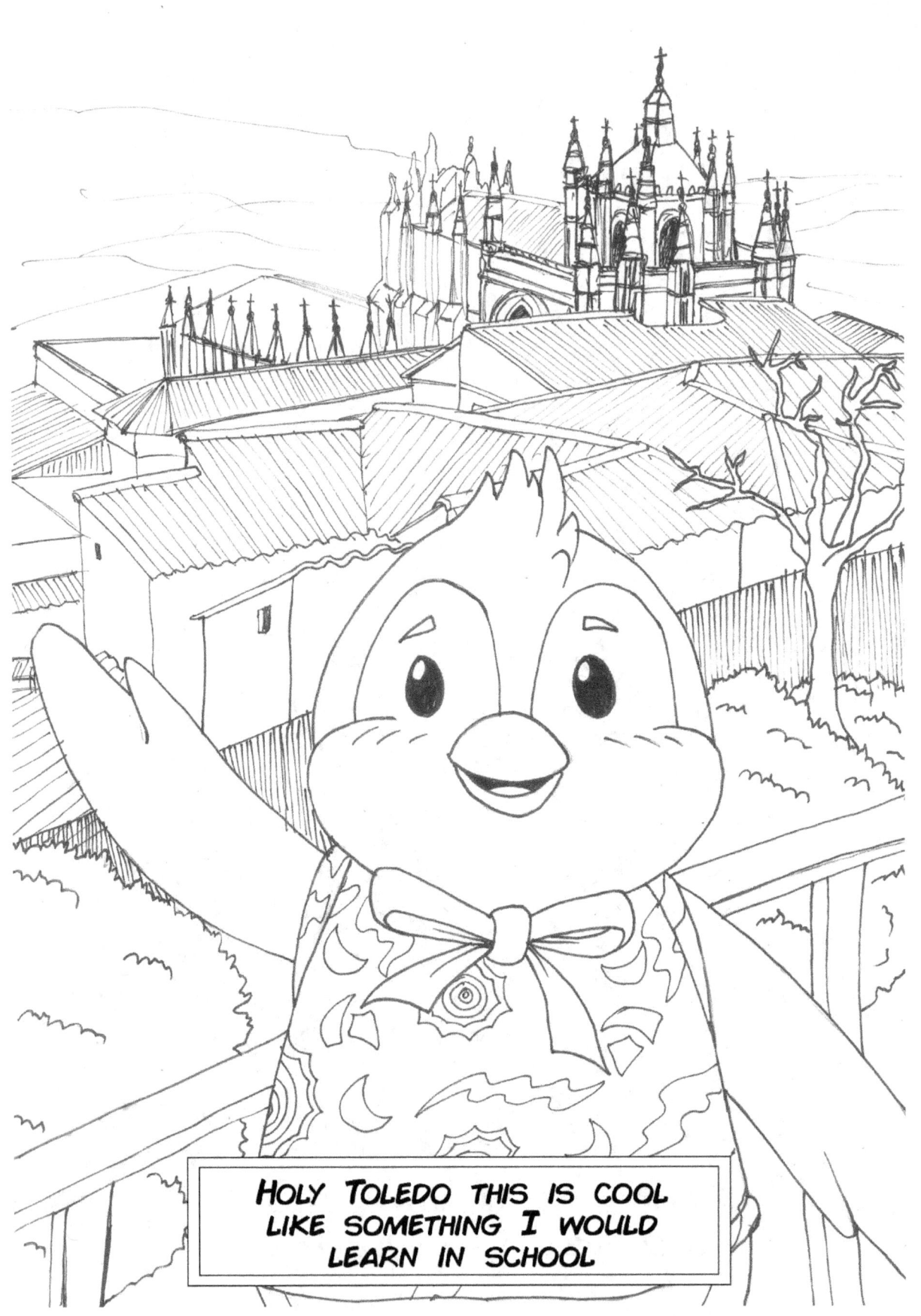

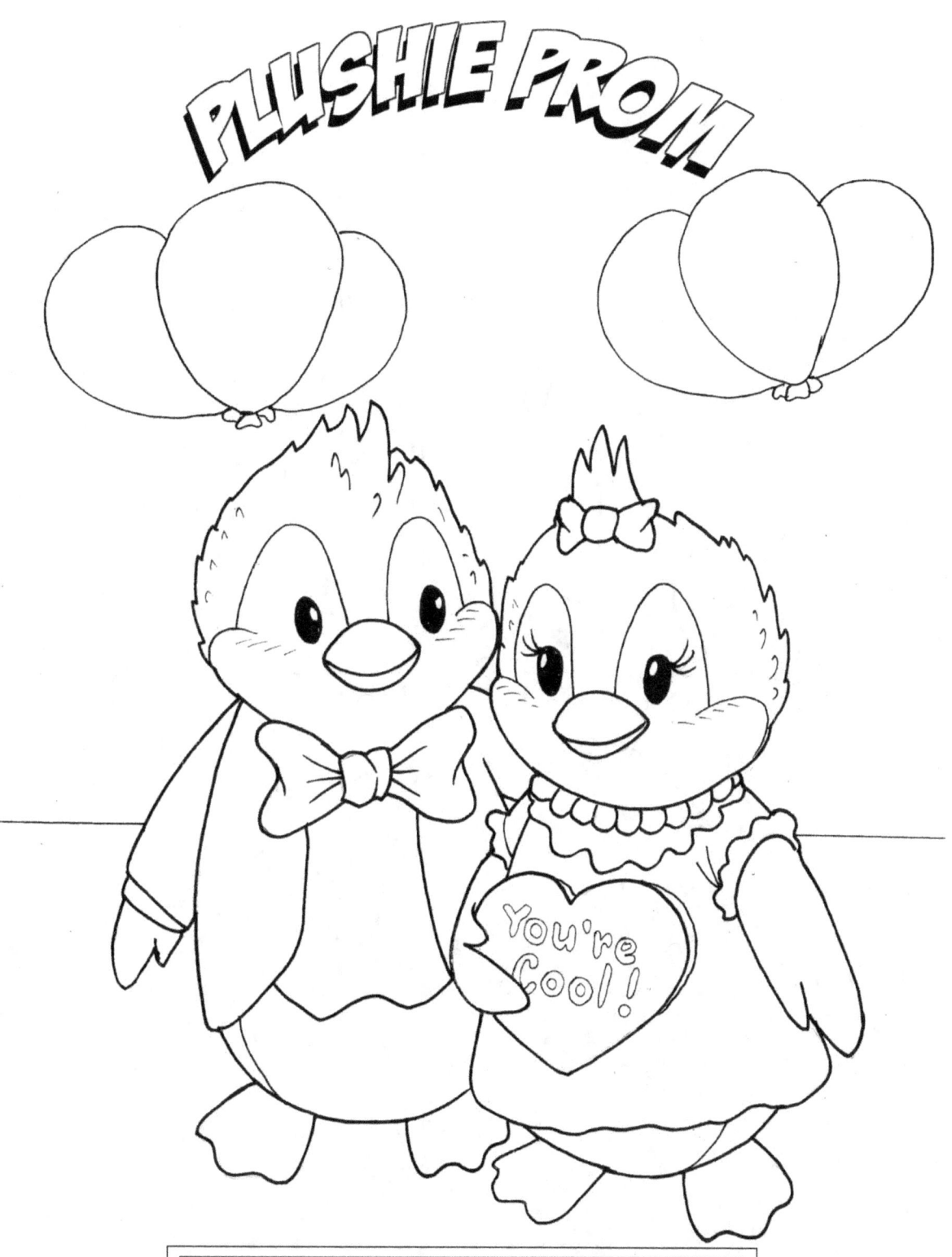

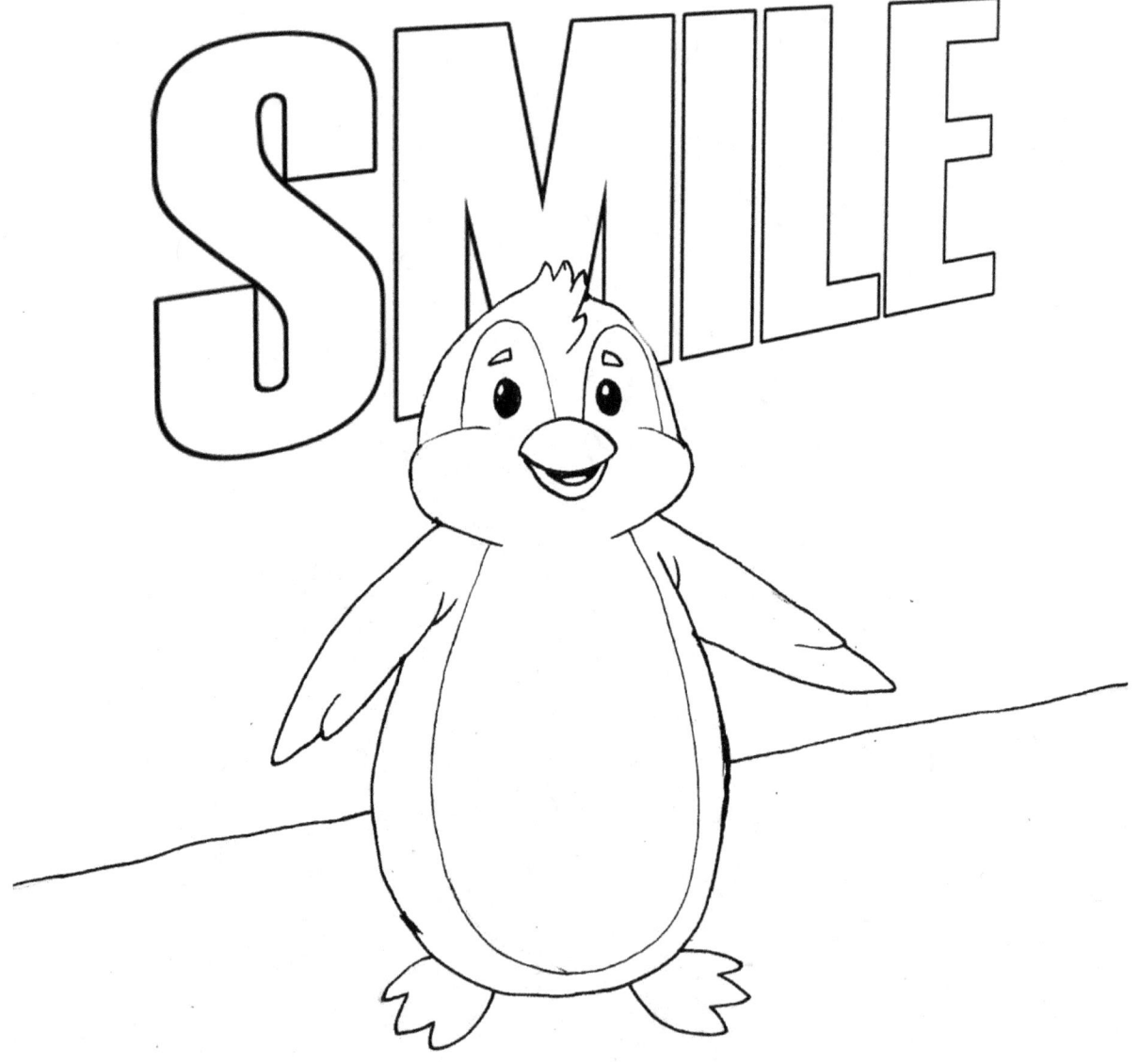

I LIKE TO SMILE TO BRING SOME CHEER I AM GRINNING FROM EAR TO EAR

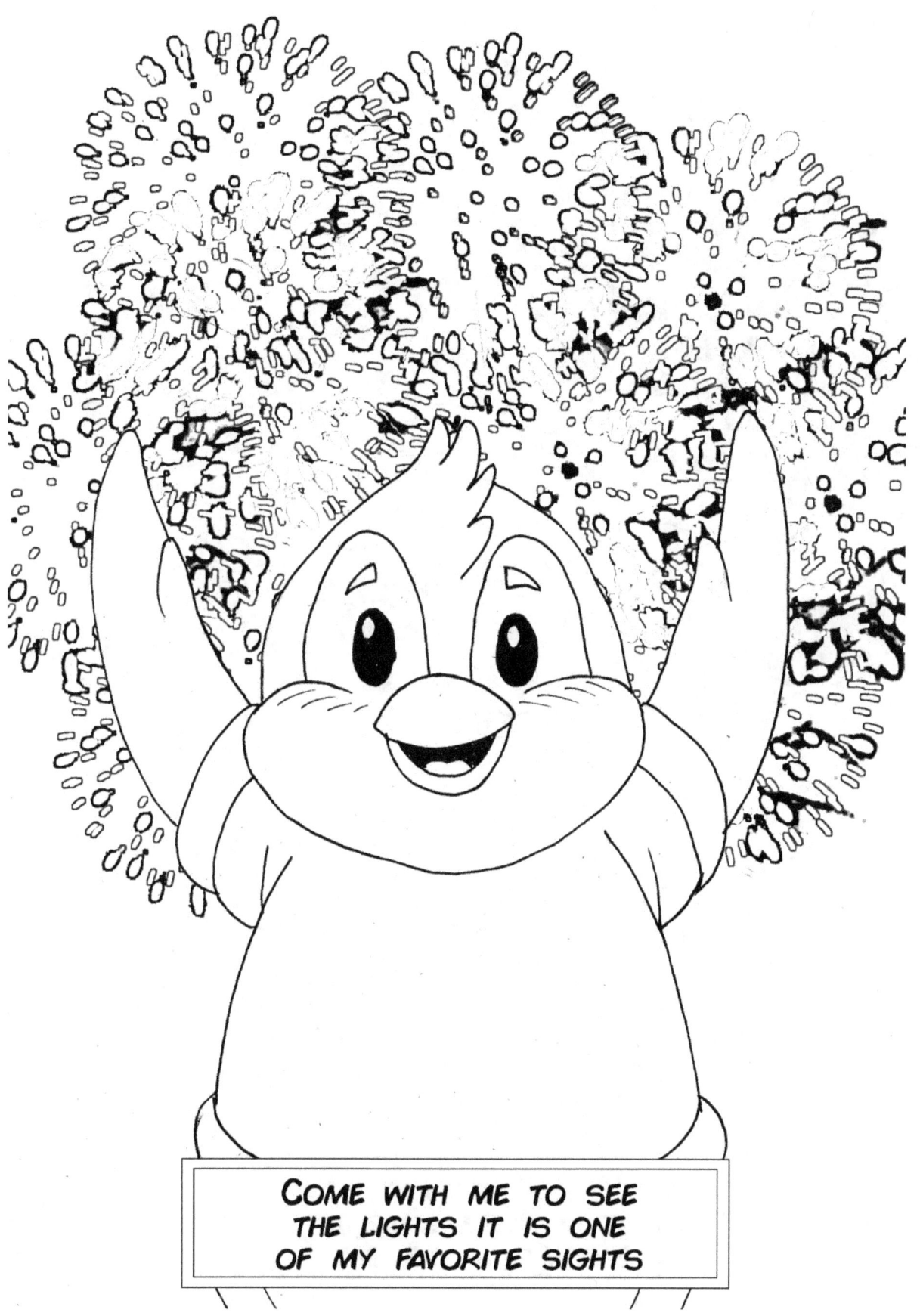

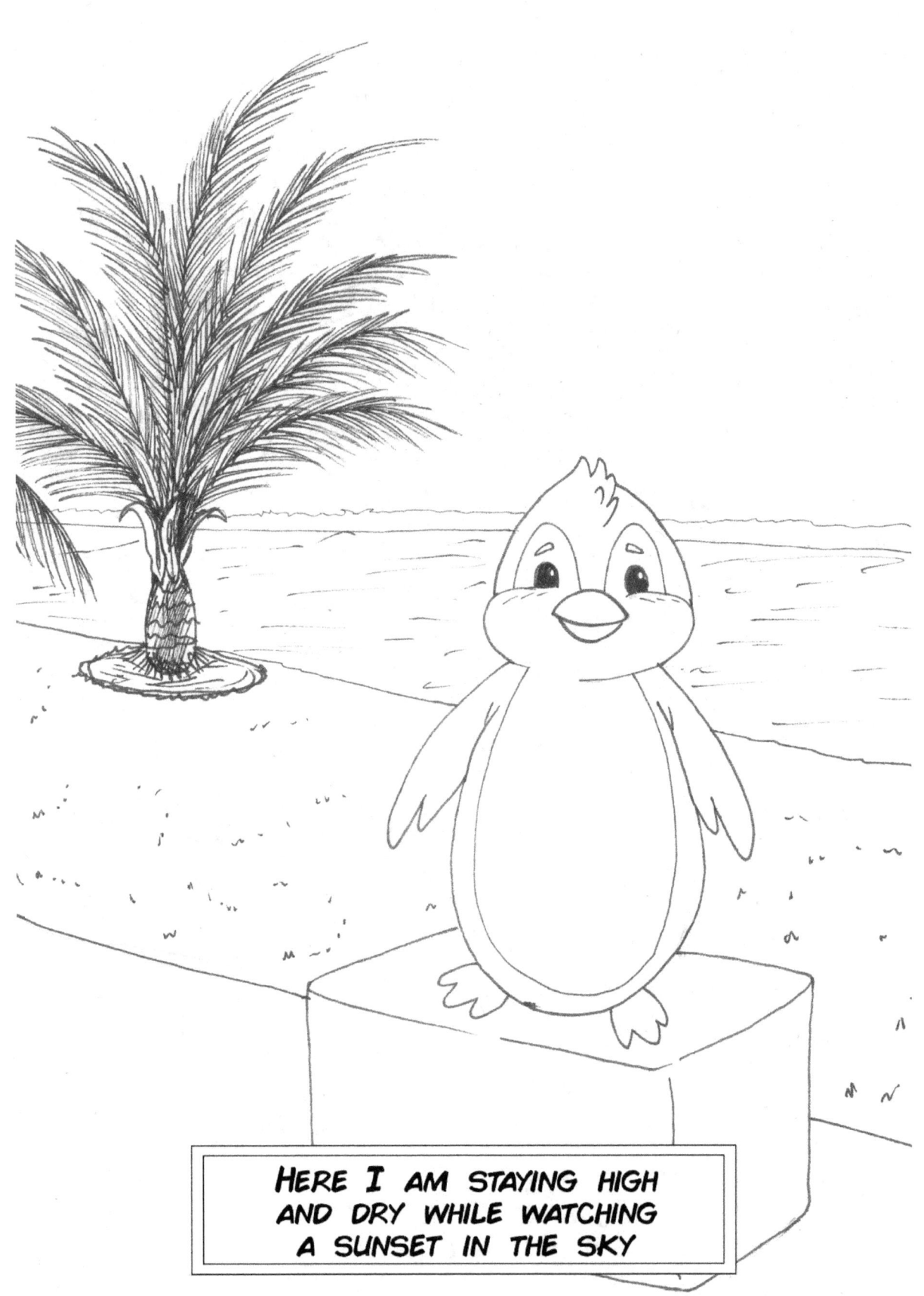

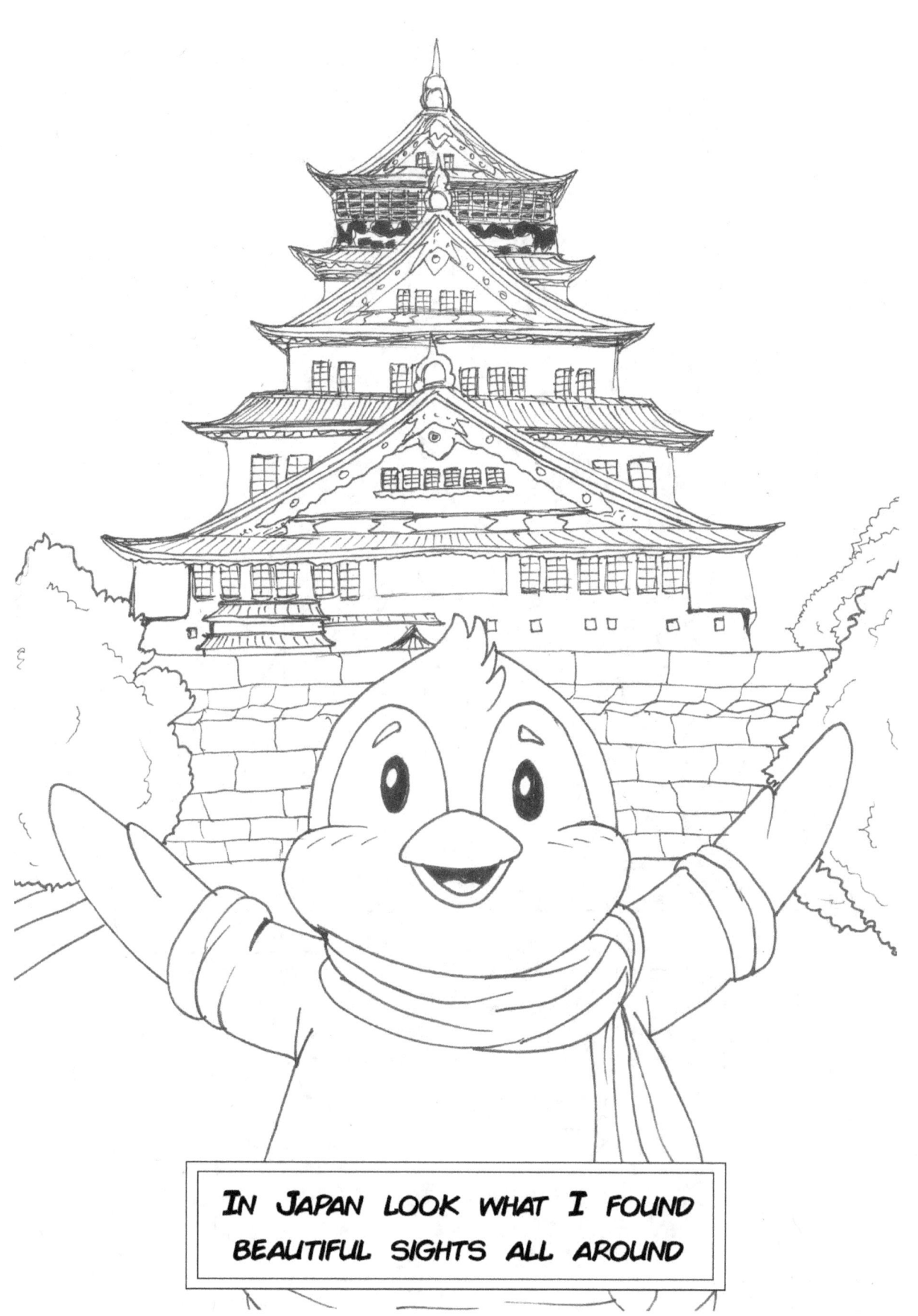

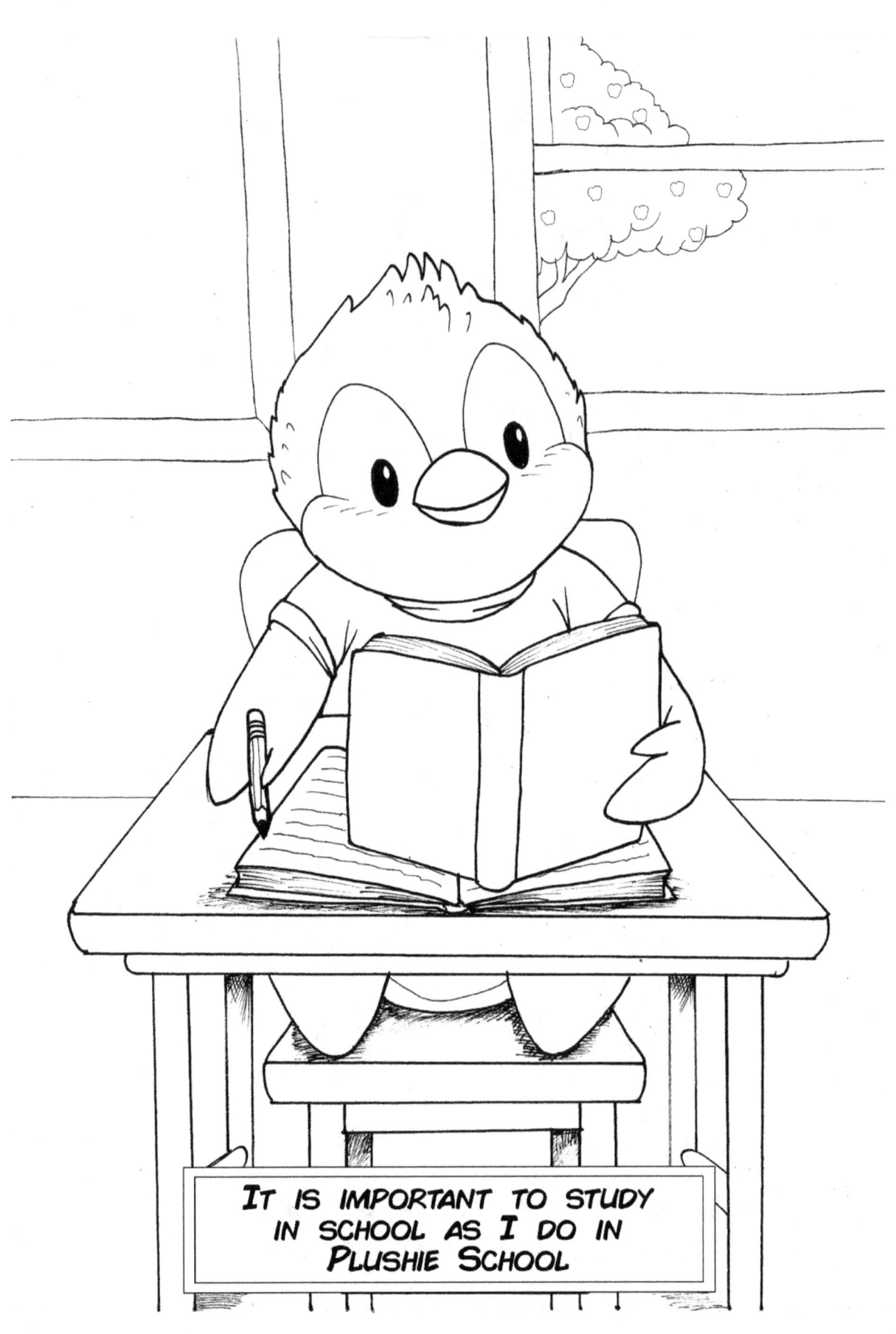

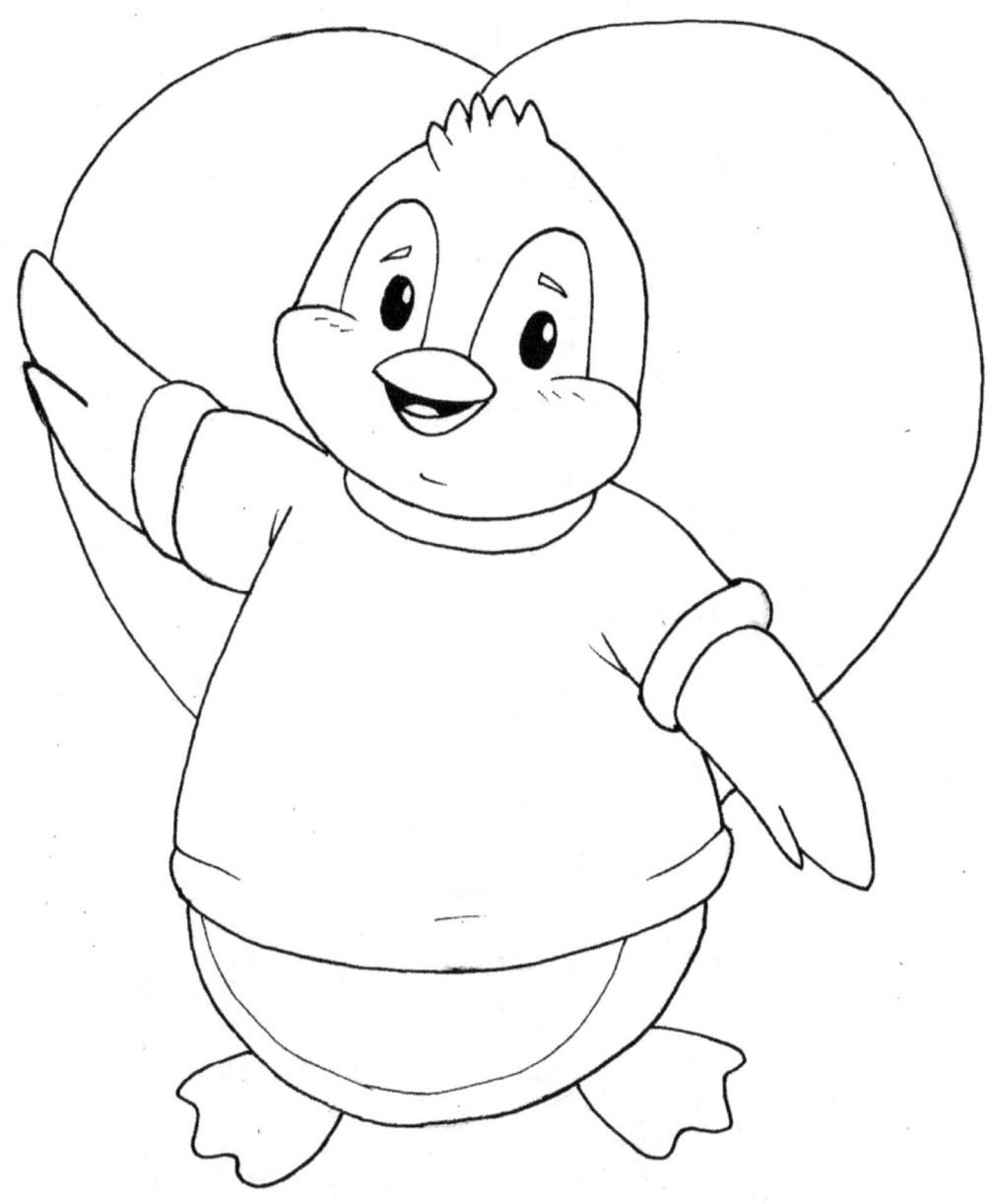

I WANT TO SHOW YOU
A PIECE OF MY HEART
TO SHOW YOU WE ARE
NEVER FAR APART

www.ingramcontent.com/pod-product-compliance
Lightning Source LLC
Chambersburg PA
CBHW052043280526
45791CB00010B/3068